FY 95 Reading
Improvement Program

A New True Book

THE MANDANS

By Emilie U. Lepthien

CHILDRENS PRESS®

CHICAGO

A Mandan at the Little Shell Powwow

To my teachers at Portage Park Elementary School, Chicago, Illinois, especially Miss Elizabeth Crosby and the late Cora K. Schultz

PHOTO CREDITS

The Bettmann Archive—12, 27

© Reinhard Brucker—7 (bottom right), 10 (3 photos), 15 (top center), 16 (2 photos), 20 (bottom), 21 (2 photos), 25, 35 (bottom), 41 (left)

Historical Pictures Service, Chicago—4 (3 photos), 7 (left), 11 (right), 23, 24, 29 (top left, bottom left & right), 30

Joslyn Art Museum, Omaha, Nebraska—31 (right)

© Emilie Lepthien—11 (left), 22 (2 photos), 26, 41 (right), 42, 43, 44 (left)

Museum of the American Indian—15 (top right)

National Anthropological Archives, Smithsonian Institution—36

National Museum of American Art, Smithsonian Institution, Gift of Mrs. Joseph Harrison, Jr—19, 20 (top), 31 (left), 33, 38

The New York Public Library—17

North Dakota Tourism Promotion—7 (top right)

North Wind Picture Archives—15 (bottom), 28 (2 photos), 29 (top right)

Photri—Cover

© Chris Roberts—45 (right)

© John Running—2, 44 (right), 45 (left)

Tom Stack & Associates—© Brian Parker, 15 (top left); © Don & Pat Valenti, 35 (inset)

Cover — Mandan War Chief with his favorite wife, painted by George Catlin in 1832

Library of Congress Cataloging-in-Publication Data

Lepthien, Emilie U. (Emilie Utteg)
   The Mandans / by Emilie U. Lepthien.
      p.   cm. — (A New true book)
   Summary: Describes the history, beliefs, customs, homes, and day-to-day life of the Mandan Indians. Also discusses how they live today.
   ISBN 0-516-01180-4
   1. Mandan—Juvenile literature.
[1. Mandan Indians.   2.   Indians of North America.]
I. Title.
E99.M2L46   1989   89-22235
973′.04975—dc20   CIP
                                      AC

TABLE OF CONTENTS

Good Bird (right),
son of Son of Star,
survived the smallpox epidemic
of 1837. The Mandan
medicine man (below)
was painted by
George Catlin. Another
artist painted the
Mandan shown below right.

THE PEACEFUL MANDANS

The Mandans called themselves "Us" or "We the People." Their name means "River Dwellers" or "Those Who Dwell by the River." They were peaceful farmers.

The Mandans have many legends. They say they were the first people on earth. They also say they first lived underground. Then they climbed up a grapevine to the surface. But the grapevine broke before

everyone reached the top.
So some of the people
stayed underground.

Those who reached
the surface were led by
Natchitak (Chief Above)
and Atna (Mother Corn).

Lone Man was their mythical
hero. They said he saved the
tribe when a great flood
covered the whole earth.
Lone Man built a wooden wall
around the tribe to protect
them from the rising water.
Natchitak saved grains of
corn underground during
the flood.

George Catlin painted this Mandan village in the 1800s.
At Slant Village visitors can see the sacred Lone Man cedar
post that was built in the center of every Mandan village.

The Mandans remembered
Lone Man by erecting a
sacred cedar post in the
center of their villages.

For centuries the Mandans
farmed the land along rivers. **7**

There are no written records of their history. But the Mandans said they were once a large and powerful nation. They said they traveled many miles and suffered many trials.

The Mandans settled along the Missouri River in what is now South Dakota, probably between 1000 and 1400 A.D. Later they built villages on the cliffs above the river in what is now North Dakota.

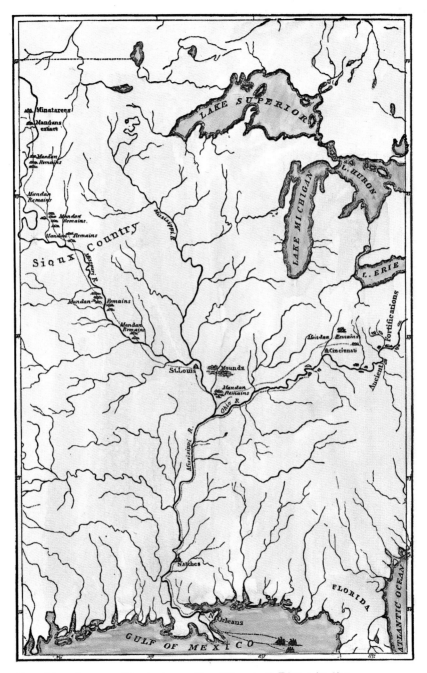

The Mandans settled along the Missouri River in the
land that is now North and South Dakota.

Bone tools and
bead necklaces made
by the Mandans

Mandan
moccasins

A HUNTING AND FARMING PEOPLE

The women tilled the soil with buffalo shoulder bones. They planted corn, squash, beans, and sunflowers.

The women worked hard. They carried water up to the village. They cooked over the fire in the center of their earth lodges. They made cups, pitchers, and pots from clay they baked in little kilns in the hillsides.

The Mandans grew sunflowers (left) for food. The women (right) pounded corn into meal.

They cut strips of buffalo
meat and dried them in the
sun to make jerky. They
pounded parched corn into meal.
Mixed with fat, the cornmeal
was formed into small balls.
These could be boiled or eaten
uncooked on hunting trips.

The women tanned buffalo
and deer skins to make
clothing.
Bullboats shaped like
round tubs were made from

Mandan women carry buffalo-hide boats to the river.

raw buffalo hides stretched on willow branches. The women stood up in the bullboats as they paddled down the river with extra crops to trade.

Animal horns were made into ladles. Flint was used to make knives. Later the Mandans traded with fur traders for metal kettles and knives.

Although the Mandan were peaceful people, they defended themselves against warring tribes. Their

weapons were spears and
bows and arrows.

They also used these in
hunting buffalo, their main
source of meat. They hunted
on foot. Hidden under wolf
skins, they crept up on the
buffalo. They took the meat
back to the village on
carriers called travois.

The buffalo hides were
used for temporary shelters
on the hunt, for snowshoes,
and for other needs.

In later times, extra crops
were traded for horses, guns,

Hidden by wolf skins, the Mandans hunted the buffalo (bison).
They skinned the animals with their knives (top center) and used the
hides to make shields (above right), robes, and many other objects.

and ammunition. That made
it easier to hunt buffalo,
deer, elk, antelope, porcupine,
wolf, and beaver.

Exterior and interior of a Mandan earth lodge

The men built the earth lodges. They dug down about two feet to make the floors of the lodges. They also erected the heavy poles for these lodges. The women put up the smaller posts and covered

the earth lodges with grass,

At times, horses were sheltered inside the earth lodge.

willow branches, and clay.
The earth lodges were so
well built they could be used
for eight to ten years during
hard winters.

The women owned the
lodges and the horses.

MANDAN VILLAGE LIFE

The lodges were built in a
circle. In the center of each
village stood the sacred
Lone Man post and a large
ceremonial lodge. The
chief's lodge was larger than
the others.

There were at least nine
Mandan villages, most of
them on the west bank of
the Missouri. At one time
there may have been nine
thousand Mandans.

In the winter, the people

moved to smaller lodges in the woods, where firewood was easier to gather.

The Mandans enjoyed sports and ceremonies. The Okipa ceremony lasted four days. Young men tested their endurance during the Okipa. Buffalo dances were held before a hunt.

Mandan
Bull Dance
painted by
George
Catlin

A favorite Mandan game was played with a hoop and a pole.

Game pieces for playing Sha-we

Pieces of carved stone used in a Mandan game

The Mandans worshiped nature and believed in a future life where things would be better. Some Mandans believed the soul, or spirit, returned to the underground home from which their ancestors climbed.

RELATIONS WITH OTHER TRIBES

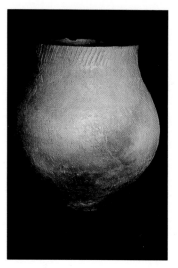

Hidatsa
pot

Both the Mandans and
the Hidatsa spoke Siouan
languages. The Hidatsa also

Hidatsa flute used for courting

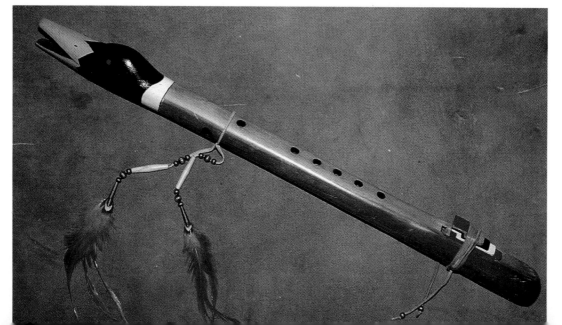

Hidatsa earth lodge at Knife River (left). Like the Mandan, the Hidatsa planted corn, squash, beans, and sunflowers.

were farmers. They built earth lodges in small villages. Some people once called this tribe Gros Ventre.

Later the Arikara, another farming tribe, arrived on the Missouri River. They spoke a Caddoan language.

Pierre La Vérendrye, a
French Canadian, visited the
Mandan villages in 1738.
Soon other explorers and fur
traders followed.

The Lewis and Clark Expedition enters a Mandan village.

THE LEWIS AND CLARK EXPEDITION

There were five Mandan and Hidatsa villages with a population of about 4,400 when the Lewis and Clark Expedition arrived there in October 1804. The explorers built a fort across the river

Fort Mandan

from the Mandans. To honor
their Native American friends,
they named it Fort Mandan.

The American Indians—and
especially the Mandans—
helped the Lewis and Clark
Expedition. The Mandans
were very generous. They
gave Lewis and Clark corn

A statue of Sacagawea stands in Bismarck, the capital of North Dakota.

for the winter. They also told them about the land farther up the Missouri River.

A Hidatsa war party had captured Sacagawea (Bird Woman), a Shoshoni girl, in 1800. In 1804, when Lewis

and Clark met her, she was
married to Toussaint
Charbonneau, a Canadian
trapper, and had a baby.
Lewis and Clark hired
Charbonneau as a guide.
They knew Sacagawea
would be especially helpful.
Charbonneau, Sacagawea,
and their baby, Jean Baptiste,

Sacagawea as painted by N. C. Wyeth

traveled all the way to the Pacific Ocean with Lewis and Clark and back to the Hidatsa village.

Lewis and Clark wrote down many Mandan and Hidatsa words. They kept journals that tell much about these tribes.

Clark took notes and made drawings of the different plants and animals he saw.

PICTORIAL RECORDS

The artist George Catlin spent several weeks with the Mandans in 1832. He painted many pictures of Mandan village life.

George Catlin (1796-1872) painted the Mandans. He spent years visiting and painting the Native Americans of North America.

Maximilian and Bodmer met the Minnetree chiefs at Fort Clark.

In 1833-1834, Alexander Philip Maximilian and Karl Bodmer, an artist, visited the tribes. The paintings of Bodmer and Catlin are an important record of these peaceful tribes. Maximilian's written records are also important.

The most famous Mandan chief was Four Bears. Catlin had high praise for the chief's friendship, generosity, and bravery.

Catlin's painting of Four Bears (left) and Bodmer's painting of Flying War Eagle (below)

TRAGEDY

In 1837, the Arikaras
joined the Mandans and
Hidatsa. Several times the
three tribes had caught
smallpox from traders. Deaths
from smallpox had greatly
reduced the Arikara tribe. The
other two tribes had also
lost many members. But
the smallpox epidemic of
1837 was a major tragedy.
An American Fur Company

George Catlin painted this view of the Missouri River about 600 miles north of St. Louis.

boat came up the Missouri.
A man on board had smallpox.
When the steamer stopped
for trading, the Indians
caught the disease. There
was no vaccine available.
Only 125 Mandans survived

the epidemic. They had
stayed in their villages for
fear of a Sioux attack. The
Hidatsa and Arikara
scattered. Still, half of their
members died also.

Chief Four Bears, dying of
smallpox, told everyone that
the men he had thought were
his friends were his worst
enemies.

When the epidemic was
over, the Mandans and
Hidatsa joined and moved
up to Like-a-Fishhook bend
on the Missouri River in

The Mandans built their villages where there was water and plenty of game, such as buffalo. Slant Village was built near the Missouri River.

1844. The land was fertile. There were trees and wild game. So the Mandans and Hidatsa built an earth-lodge village on a cliff overlooking the river in 1845.

35

Fort Clark was built on the Missouri River.

FUR TRADING

The Mandans had been
fur trading with the North
West Company since 1794.
Other fur traders followed.
The American Fur Company

built a post south of Fort Mandan. They called it Fort Clark. Then in 1845 the company moved to a new fort at Like-a-Fishhook bend near the earth-lodge village.

By 1846 the fort was called Fort Berthold. The Fort Laramie Treaty of 1851 assigned boundaries for the territory held by the Hidatsa and Mandan tribes and the Arikaras. The Hidatsa chief attended the council.

By 1862, the three tribes were completely joined.

American Indians on buffalo-hide snowshoes hunted the buffalo.

They were called the Three Affiliated Tribes.

Cholera epidemics, a decrease in wild game, drought, floods, and frost plagued them. The Sioux continued to attack the village.

THE FORT BERTHOLD RESERVATION

The Fort Berthold Reservation was established for the three tribes in 1870 to guarantee the American Indians possession of their land. Nevertheless, by 1886 the three tribes had lost about 90 percent of their land. Game was soon gone and the Indians were hungry most of the year. Gradually families abandoned their earth lodges near Like-a-

Fishhook bend. The three tribes began to move into different sections of the reservation. The Arikaras settled in the eastern part, the Mandans south and west of the Missouri, and the Hidatsa near Elbowoods and Salt Creek and with the Mandans. Small villages were established.

Churches and schools were built. Indian language and culture were changing. But another drastic change was to occur.

GARRISON DAM

In 1946, construction was begun on Garrison Dam on the Missouri River. The dam is thirty miles downstream from the eastern boundary of the Fort Berthold reservation. The dam was completed in 1956. The resulting reservoir, called Lake Sakakawea, flooded

Garrison Dam power plant (left) and generating station (right)

Because of Lake Sakakawea, seven reservation schools had to be relocated. New homes and new roads had to be built.

25 percent of the reservation. The waters covered the land where the three tribes farmed and where they cut timber.

Ninety percent of the people had to move. Their livelihood was taken away. They had to find new ways in which to earn a living.

TRIBAL GOVERNMENT

Mandaree, Fort Berthold Reservation

The reservation is divided into six segments. One member of the Tribal Council is elected from each segment. The chairman is from the Tribal Business Council. The headquarters for the tribe is in New Town, east of Four Bears Bridge.

There are over 8,000 enrolled members of the Three Affiliated Tribes. But less than 3,200 live on the

43

Elementary school and high school
at Mandaree (above) and Mandan clan brothers
at the Little Shell Powwow
at Fort Berthold, North Dakota (right)

reservation. Most of them
live in the communities of
Mandaree, White Shield,
Twin Buttes, Drags Wolf,
Parshall, and New Town.

Indian culture and tribal
history are taught in the
schools. Arikara language
classes are given in the Fort
Berthold College Center.

44

The traditions of the Mandan, Hidatsa, and Arikara people are kept alive by the young.

Today, the Mandans as a separate tribe have all but disappeared. But, together with the Hidatsa and the Arikara, they remind us of the contribution the Native Americans made to our heritage. **45**

WORDS YOU SHOULD KNOW

affiliated(uh • FILL • ee • ait • id) — joined; associated

Caddoan(KAD • oh • in) — a family of American Indian languages spoken by peoples of the Great Plains

ceremonial(sair • ih • MOAN • ee • yal) — used for celebrations or religious services

cholera(KAHL • er • ah) — a disease that spreads quickly and is often fatal

earth lodge(ERTH LAHJ) — a home made from a frame of wooden posts set in the earth and covered with branches, grass, and clay

earthen(ER • thin) — made from baked clay

endurance(en • DOO • rens) — the ability to work or exercise for a long time without tiring

epidemic(ep • pih • DEM • ick) — an outbreak of disease in which many people become ill

expedition(ex • pih • DIH • shun) — an organized trip, usually of a large party, for a purpose such as exploration or discovery

floodplain(FLUD • playne) — the land near a river that becomes flooded when the river overflows

jerky(JER • kee) — meat cut into strips and preserved by drying in the sun

kiln(KIHLN) — an oven used to heat and harden pottery

mythical(MIH • thih • kil) — like a myth; heroic

parched(PARCHT) — roasted or toasted with dry heat

reservoir(REZ • er • vwahr) — an artificial lake that forms behind a dam

sacred(SAY • krid) —holy; set apart for some religious reason

Siouan(SOO • an) —a group of American Indian languages spoken by peoples of central and eastern North America

tan(TAN) —to soften and preserve an animal skin; to make leather

travois(tra • VOY) —a device for carrying loads, made of two poles that trail on the ground behind a dog or horse, with a net or platform between them

vaccine(vack • SEEN) —a substance given to people to help them fight off a disease

INDEX

About the Author

Emilie Utteg Lepthien earned a BS and MA Degree and certificate in school administration from Northwestern University. She taught third grade, upper grade science and social studies, and was a supervisor and principal of Wicker Park School for twenty years. Mrs. Lepthien has also written and narrated science and social studies scripts for the Radio Council (WBEZ) of the Chicago Board of Education.

Mrs. Lepthien was awarded the American Educator's Medal by Freedoms Foundation. She is a member of Delta Kappa Gamma Society International, Illinois Women's Press Association, National Federation of Press Women, Iota Sigma Epsilon Journalism sorority, Chicago Principals Association, and is active in church work. She has co-authored primary social studies books for Rand, McNally and Company and served as educational consultant for Encyclopaedia Britannica Films.